T0080645

WORLD WINDOWS

Ways to Travel

HEINLE
CENGAGE Learning™

Y|S|G
A YBM COMPANY
Young & Son
Global, Inc.

How do you get to school?

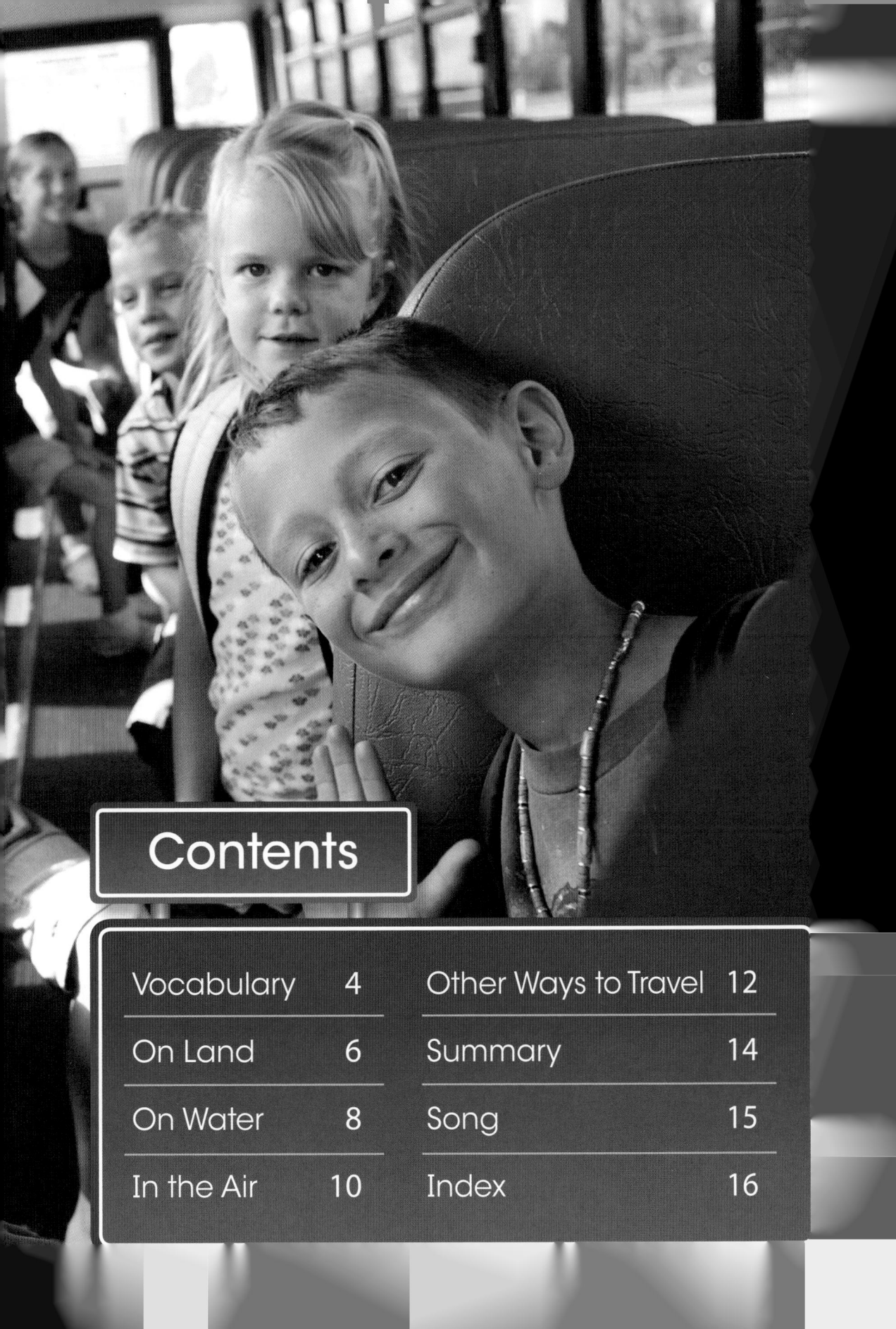

Contents

Vocabulary	4	Other Ways to Travel	12
On Land	6	Summary	14
On Water	8	Song	15
In the Air	10	Index	16

Vocabulary
ship
sailboat

airplane
helicopter
car
train

People travel on land by car.

People travel on land by train.

People travel on water by ship.

People travel on water by sailboat.

People travel in the air by airplane.

People travel in the air by helicopter.

bicycle

bus

People travel every day.

balloon

canoe

People get from place to place in many ways.

Summary

How do people travel?

Song

Watch It Go!

Watch the car go by land,
Go by land, go by land.
Watch the car go by land,
To get from place to place!

Watch the ship go by water,
Go by water, go by water.
Watch the ship go by water,
To get from place to place!

Watch the airplane go by air,
Go by air, go by air.
Watch the airplane go by air,
To get from place to place!

Index

air, 10–11

airplane, 10

balloon, 13

bicycle, 12

bus, 12

canoe, 13

car, 6

helicopter, 11

land, 6–7

sailboat, 9

ship, 8

train, 7

water, 8–9